S0-ACD-425

THE **REAL** STORY:
DEBUNKING HISTORY

THE REAL STORY BEHIND THE

13 COLONIES

CHRISTINE HONDERS

PowerKiDS press

New York

Published in 2020 by The Rosen Publishing Group, Inc.
29 East 21st Street, New York, NY 10010

Copyright © 2020 by The Rosen Publishing Group, Inc.

All rights reserved. No part of this book may be reproduced in any form without permission in writing from the publisher, except by a reviewer.

First Edition

Editor: Jill Keppeler
Book Design: Reann Nye

Photo Credits: Cover SuperStock/Getty Images; p. 5, Courtesy of the Library of Congress; pp. 7, 9 (bottom), 25 Universal History Archive/ Universal Images Group/Getty Images; p. 9 (top) https://commons.wikimedia.org/wiki/File:Castillo_de_San_Marcos_Fort_Panorama_1.jpg; p. 11 https://commons.wikimedia.org/wiki/File:John_Smith_taking_the_King_of_Pamavnkee_prisoner_-_etching.jpg; p. 13 Kean Collection / Hulton Fine Art Collection/Getty Images; p. 14 Archive Photos/Getty Images; p. 15 Lambert/ Hulton Fine Art Collection/Getty Images; pp. 16, 21 Bettmann/Getty Images; p. 17 Science & Society Picture Library/Getty Images; p. 19 Library of Congress/Corbis Historical/Getty Images; p. 23 https://commons.wikimedia.org/wiki/File:Dutch_soldiers_in_a_boat_with_slaves_from_the_Colonies,_Africa_(NYPL_b14896507-95335).tiff; p. 26 https://commons.wikimedia.org/wiki/File:Constitution_of_the_United_States,_page_1.jpg; p. 27 Three Lions/Hulton Archive/Getty Images; p. 29 (top) ttps://commons.wikimedia.org/wiki/File:John_Singleton_Copley_001.jpg; p. 29 (bottom) https://commons.wikimedia.org/wiki/File:Sir_Joshua_Reynolds_-_John_Murray,_4th_Earl_of_Dunmore_-_Google_Art_Project.jpg.

Cataloging-in-Publication Data

Names: Honders, Christine.
Title: The real story behind the 13 colonies / Christine Honders.
Description: New York : PowerKids Press, 2020. | Series: The real story: debunking history | Includes glossary and index.
Identifiers: ISBN 9781538344668 (pbk.) | ISBN 9781538343456 (library bound) | ISBN 9781538344675 (6 pack)
Subjects: LCSH: United States–History–Colonial period, ca. 1600-1775–Juvenile literature.
Classification: LCC E188.H66 2020 | DDC 973.2–dc23

Manufactured in the United States of America

CPSIA Compliance Information: Batch #CSPK19. For Further Information contact Rosen Publishing, New York, New York at 1-800-237-9932

CONTENTS

THE THANKSGIVING MYTH

We've all read or heard the story of the first Thanksgiving. The Pilgrims landed on Plymouth Rock, Massachusetts, in 1620, or so the story goes. After their first successful harvest in 1621, they held a celebration feast and invited the local Indians to join them. This became a tradition they named "Thanksgiving."

Much of this, however, may not be true. Plymouth Rock wasn't mentioned in the settlers' writings. The historic feast wasn't called "Thanksgiving" until the 1830s. There's no evidence that the Indians were invited. And the meal likely didn't even include turkey!

This story isn't the only fun-but-somewhat-fictional tale people have learned about the first British colonies in North America. Not everything we've heard or been taught about the 13 colonies that became the United States is real.

GOOD SOURCES

Many stories can be fun or interesting—but just because something's fun doesn't mean it's true. Check your sources before you believe a story about U.S. history or anything else. How do you know if that Internet article is a good source? Check the author. Do they know a lot about their field? Look at the article's sources. Where did the author get their information? Search for more information if you're unsure.

Pilgrims didn't wear tall hats with buckles on them. Later artists painted them that way because they thought it looked old fashioned.

THE WHOLE STORY

Sometimes school textbooks don't tell the whole story. Many history books about the 13 colonies just include the colonists' point of view and don't include the **perspective** of the Native Americans they killed or the Africans they enslaved. Unpleasant, **brutal** facts about how the Europeans settled in North America are often left out so that we have a more positive view of our country's history.

You may have been told that many of the people who first came to the New World were escaping religious **persecution**. While religion did influence many colonists, they didn't intend to come here and establish freedom of religion for all. The Puritans in particular wanted to establish their religion and force everyone to follow it. They only wanted freedom for themselves.

FACT FINDER

English leaders, who didn't want to lose their best merchants and farmers, discouraged people from moving to the New World by telling them that the only people going there were criminals running away from punishment.

FOUNDING THE THIRTEEN

The 13 British colonies that became the United States were Virginia, Massachusetts, New Hampshire, Maryland, Connecticut, Rhode Island, Delaware, North Carolina, South Carolina, New Jersey, New York, Pennsylvania, and Georgia. Virginia was the first to be established when Jamestown was founded in 1607, but it didn't become a royal colony until 1624. In 1732, Georgia was the last to be established. It became a royal colony in 1752.

6

Europeans settled on Roanoke Island, off the coast of modern-day North Carolina, twice, once in 1585 and again in 1587. Both times, the captains who left the island to get more supplies from England came back and found the colony abandoned. No one is sure what happened to the colonists.

FOR PRAYER OR FOR PROFIT?

Religion played a big part when Europeans created the colonies—but money was an even bigger factor. The king of England gave **charters** to people to start colonies. The charters declared that the king (or other wealthy men in England) owned the land and that they were entitled to most of the profits. In the early days of colonization, the colonists weren't interested in being free from England. They accepted that the king was in charge.

The colonists brought their habits and **culture** to a new place, but most of them weren't interested in a new way of life. They wanted the colonies to be like England in many ways. They weren't expecting to find people with a different way of life already living in their New World.

THE REAL "NEW" WORLD

The colonists weren't coming to empty lands. In some places, there were heavily populated villages in North America. The Native Americans had their own languages and laws. In many cases, they believed in community and cooperation. Giving to others was a way to earn respect. The colonists didn't understand the Native Americans' way of life. Many believed that because the natives weren't Christians, it was the colonists' religious duty to either convert them or wipe them out.

Florida was settled in 1565 by Spanish explorer Pedro Menéndez de Avilés, long before the Pilgrims arrived. His settlement, Saint Augustine, is the oldest continually populated European settlement in the United States. Above, Castillo de San Marcos is the oldest masonry fort in the continental United States.

< PEDRO MENÉNDEZ DE AVILÉS

9

A CLASH OF CULTURES

The first successful English settlement in North America was established in 1607 in what's now Virginia. This settlement, called Jamestown, was built on Pamunkey Indian land. The Pamunkeys were part of a group called the Powhatans, led by a chief of the same name. The relationship between the natives and the settlers varied. The Pamunkeys sometimes shared their food with the colonists, who didn't know how to hunt or farm well, or traded with them. But tensions grew and fighting often broke out.

While textbooks often make the Native Americans appear needlessly violent, there's evidence that the Pamunkeys tried to live in peace with the colonists. But the settlers were demanding and took the natives' attempts to listen to the colonists as signs of agreement with their ways.

The English began to push the natives from
their lands and, in 1622, the Powhatan Indians
attacked Jamestown and other settlements,
killing more than 300 of the 1,200 or so
colonists. The Powhatans may have expected
the English to leave or draw back afterward,
but instead, the conflicts became worse.

THE PROBLEM WITH POCAHONTAS

Many people have heard the story of Pocahontas. This much is true: Pocahontas was the daughter of Powhatan. The story says that the Powhatan people captured Captain John Smith, a leader of the Jamestown colony, and Powhatan ordered him to be killed. However, the story goes, Pocahontas (often called "an Indian princess") begged her father to spare Smith's life, and the natives released him. Many of the stories include a romance between Smith and Pocahontas.

Historians now aren't sure that Pocahontas ever rescued Smith and, in fact, she might have barely known him. Smith never mentioned Pocahontas in his early writings; he started adding her to his story after she visited England and became popular there. When Smith led the colony, Pocahontas would have been very young, much younger than Smith.

A TOOL FOR THE ENGLISH

Why do people like to believe the myth of Pocahontas? The colony supporters backed the popular stories because they wanted to keep the colony profitable and needed people back in England to support it. The English also liked the idea that Pocahontas's supposed love or affection for Smith showed that the Native Americans admired English culture and wanted to be like them. It may have made them feel better about their own history.

Pocahontas married a colonist named John Rolfe and visited England. She died at age 21 before she could return to North America.

13

THE PILGRIMS ARRIVE

There are probably more myths about the Pilgrims, who established the first permanent colony in the New England region, than there are about any other colonists. The story is told that the Pilgrims fled England because they wanted to be free to worship the way they wanted.

In reality, only about a third of the Pilgrims who landed in 1620 were Puritans who wanted to practice their own religion. And these Puritans had a good deal of religious freedom in Holland, where they settled in 1609 after first leaving England. The reason they later came to the New World was very similar to the reason colonists settled Jamestown: they wanted to make money. They had no interest in religious freedom for anyone else and banned other religions in their colony.

FACT FINDER

Pilgrims are usually pictured wearing black and looking solemn and ready to lecture anyone for having fun. But Edward Winslow, a colony leader, described a harvest festival in 1621 with sports, shooting, and beer.

EDWARD WINSLOW

The stories say that the Pilgrims' ship, the *Mayflower*, landed on Plymouth Rock. However, the Pilgrims never mention Plymouth Rock in their writings. And every good sailor knows to avoid a rocky coastline.

RIGHTS AND FORCE

While much of the classic Thanksgiving story is doubtful, the Pilgrims did sign a peace treaty with the Wampanoag Indians in 1621. The Indians taught the colonists how to plant, hunt, and survive. But the Pilgrims didn't trust the Indians, believing that they were savages and devil worshippers. The peace didn't last long.

More Puritans arrived in 1630 to set up the Massachusetts Bay Colony, taking over more native lands. The colony's leader, John Winthrop, said that the natives had a "natural right" to the land, but not a "civil right," under English law, because they hadn't developed it. The colonists also used Bible passages to justify taking the land by force. Over time, they created cities, including Boston and Charlestown, on this land.

JOHN WINTHROP

John Carver was the first governor of the Pilgrim settlement in Plymouth. He established a peace treaty between the Wampanoag Chief Massasoit and King James of England.

SALEM WITCH TRIALS

Everyone knows the story of the Salem witch trials, right? Some of what you think is true might not be. In 1692, starting in Salem village (today's Danvers, Massachusetts) in the Massachusetts Bay Colony, two girls began acting oddly, screaming and having fits. The local doctor, unable to find an answer, blamed witchcraft. The girls accused three women of bewitching them, and then the charges spread. Soon, dozens of people (mostly women) were accused of witchcraft—not just in Salem but throughout the colony.

Not all of these so-called witches were executed. A special court found about 200 people guilty and 19 people (four of them men) were killed. This was nothing new, however—thousands of people were executed for witchcraft throughout Europe from the 1300s to the 1600s.

FACT FINDER

People tend to believe that the "witches" found guilty during the trials were burned at the stake. However, most hanged. One, an elderly man, was pressed to death by stones.

This picture shows the 1692 trial of George Jacobs, who was one of the relatively few men accused of witchcraft in Salem. Jacobs was later one of the four men executed.

THIS LAND WAS OUR LAND

While the settlers often considered the Native Americans savages, the reality is that the Puritans (and other invaders) were often quite savage toward the original inhabitants of the continent. In the 1630s, colonists began settling in what's now Connecticut. At first, those colonists coexisted with the neighboring Pequot Indians, but they also wanted the Pequots' land. In 1636, after some Pequots killed a troublesome colonist, the English declared an all-out war.

The Pequot War lasted about a year. The colonists avoided fighting Indian warriors, preferring to burn down their villages in the middle of the night and slaughter the women and children. The colonists also convinced other Indian tribes to join them against the Pequots and then turned against those tribes. Hundreds of the Pequot people were killed in the war.

There were **massacres** and many deaths on both sides of the many conflicts between colonists and Native Americans. However, the colonists were the invaders on this continent, something history books often leave out.

SETTING THE STAGE FOR SLAVERY

There are many stories about slavery in the English colonies, but many are untrue. When the first colonies were still young, the colonists struggled to grow enough food. Learning how to grow tobacco and export it to make money helped. However, they needed more people to work on the farms. Many colonists weren't used to this kind of work and were **frustrated** by it.

The colonists couldn't enslave enough Native Americans. The colonists brought white servants from England, but there weren't enough of them, and after a few years' work they were free. By then, Spain and Portugal had enslaved and sent almost 1 million Africans to their colonies in the Caribbean and South America. The North American colonists soon turned to slavery as well.

FACT FINDER

The first Africans in Jamestown were not slaves. They were indentured servants who were freed when their duties were complete. In 1641, Massachusetts became the first state to make slavery legal.

IRISH IN AMERICA

One persistent myth about slavery in the colonies is that there were also Irish slaves. While people did sometimes call Irish immigrants "white slaves" in the 1600s and 1700s, most were in fact **indentured servants** who came to the colonies willingly. Although some were put into servitude (and taken to the colonies) against their will, indentured servitude was still temporary, and servants had rights. It also wasn't **hereditary**.

22

The Dutch played a large part
in the slave trade, transporting
about 600,000 Africans to islands
in the Caribbean, where they were
shipped to Spanish colonies.

FROM SERVANT TO SLAVE

The colonies continued to grow. The growth of **plantations** in the southern colonies of Virginia, Maryland, and the Carolinas created a desire for more slaves. Slave ships carried Africans, chained together like cattle, into the New World in horrible conditions.

However, before the American Revolution, slavery existed in every colony, even in the North. New York and Boston had large slave populations working as household servants and in many other jobs. In fact, 14 percent of the population of New York was made up of slaves in 1750. The colonies didn't start **abolishing** slavery until Vermont did so in 1777, after the Revolution had started. Some attitudes started to change because the colonists saw that their own fight for freedom **contradicted**, in many ways, the practice of slavery.

FACT FINDER

In 1781, Massachusetts (the first colony to legalize slavery) became the second state to abolish it. Still, it took years for all the slaves there to be freed.

The South had more slaves because the plantations needed so much labor to keep them running.

A REVOLUTION APPROACHES

There are many common stories about the colonies and the Revolutionary War, but not all those stories are true. There weren't even 13 colonies when the war began with the battles of Lexington and Concord in April 1775. Delaware was part of Pennsylvania (although it had its own legislature) until June 15, 1776. It broke away from the other colonies and Great Britain at the same time—and years later, it was the first state to ratify, or approve, the U.S. Constitution.

Also, the colonies didn't officially become independent on July 4, 1776. Colonial representatives voted to break away from Great Britain on July 2, 1776, and they approved the Declaration of Independence two days later. The colonies weren't truly free from Britain until the war was over and the Treaty of Paris was signed in 1783.

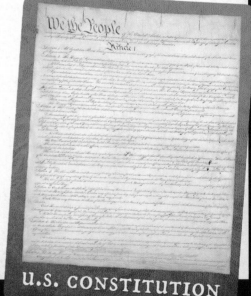

U.S. CONSTITUTION

Contrary to stories, the Liberty Bell in Philadelphia, Pennsylvania, didn't ring to mark independence on July 4, 1776. It wasn't even called the Liberty Bell until the 1830s, when it became a symbol of freedom in the antislavery movement.

SIDING WITH THE ENEMY

It's easy to believe that all the residents of all 13 colonies banded together to declare their independence against the tyrant king of England. But the truth is that not every colonist wanted to break away. Even the Founding Fathers tried to mend fences with England first. Once the war started, about a third of the colonists were Loyalists, meaning they were loyal to the king. This group included many wealthy merchants and businessmen, who didn't want the trade economy to suffer.

Some of the Loyalists fought alongside the British army. Not surprisingly, the patriots particularly hated them. In 1776, the new U.S. states passed laws raising taxes on Loyalists, taking away their property, and forbidding them to run for office. Starting in March 1776, almost 100,000 Loyalists fled the colonies.

ANOTHER FIGHT FOR FREEDOM

In 1775, Virginia royal governor John Murray, Lord Dunmore, announced that slaves who fought for the British would be freed after the war—but only slaves owned by the rebels. Hundreds of slaves joined Dunmore's Ethiopian Regiment in hopes of a new life. Dunmore wasn't interested in ending the suffering of slaves. He used this offer as a threat towards patriot slave owners. Many of the regiment's members died.

This painting shows the Battle of Jersey in January 1781. The British surrendered at Yorktown, Virginia, in October 1781, but the war actually continued for two more years.

< LORD DUNMORE

THE ORIGINAL COLONIES IN A NEW LIGHT

Why are there so many untrue or partially true stories about the English colonies? Some come from poems or songs, while others may have been **exaggerated** to give people a sense of patriotism. If people hear a story from only one point of view, they won't have a full understanding of what really happened.

Most of history has been written by the winners, the people who received the most benefit. But it's equally important to look at history through the eyes of others. What did the Native Americans think when they saw strange ships arriving on their shores? What did the first African slaves in North America see when they landed in Virginia in 1619? Do some research! The truth might surprise you.

GLOSSARY

abolish: To officially end or stop something, especially slavery.

brutal: Especially violent or severe.

charter: A document issued by a government that gives rights to a person or group.

contradict: To say the opposite of something.

culture: The beliefs and ways of life of a certain group of people.

exaggerate: To describe something as larger or better than it really is.

frustrate: To cause to feel discouraged, upset, and often angry about something.

hereditary: Passed from parent to child.

indentured servant: A person who is bound to work for another for a specific period of time, often in exchange for passage to a new country.

massacre: The violent killing of many people.

persecution: Cruel treatment, especially because of a person's race or religious or political beliefs.

perspective: Point of view.

plantation: A large farm.

INDEX

WEBSITES

Due to the changing nature of Internet links, PowerKids Press has developed an online list of websites related to the subject of this book. This site is updated regularly. Please use this link to access the list: www.powerkidslinks.com/debunk/colonies